www.finishinglinepress.com

Cloister Walk

poems by

Priscilla Melchior

Finishing Line Press
Georgetown, Kentucky

Cloister Walk

ACKNOWLEDGMENTS

Thank you to the publications in which these poems—or earlier versions of
them—first appeared.

Verse-Virtual: At the Hawk Watch; Turkey Vulture; With the Dogs in the
Woods
North Carolina Literary Review: Summer Dawn
Streetlight Magazine: Migration
Ekphrastic Review: Nighthawks

I am also grateful to those who have provided strength and encouragement
throughout my writing journey: my husband, Bill Royster; my sons,
Christian and Sam, as well as friends and mentors including members of
Poets@Large, our longtime poetry group.

Publisher: Leah Huete de Maines
Editor: Christen Kincaid
Cover Art: Priscilla Melchior
Author Photo:William F. Royster
Cover Design: Elizabeth Maines McCleavy

Order online: www.finishinglinepress.com
also available on amazon.com

Author inquiries and mail orders:
Finishing Line Press
PO Box 1626
Georgetown, Kentucky 40324
USA

Contents

For my husband, Bill, and my sons, Christian and Sam

Spellbound

I've never been a fan of magicians,
don't care when they levitate women
or pull rabbits from hats. I'm not
interested in the lies they ask me
to accept simply by labeling them
illusions.

Reality is my alchemy. The thin veil
of fog rising from a still morning pond
is far more enchanting than any *Poof!*
of smoke that comes with the sweep
of a crimson cape. No prestidigitation
compares to the mystery

of deer as they evaporate into the woods,
or the roiling approach of a thunderstorm.
So forgive me if I embrace the legerdemain
of a world with wonders of its own. I'll forgo
the sorcerer's wizardry, bewitched instead
by the miracle of everyday.

At the hawk watch

I step into their sanctuary
an outsider, curious, but
they are quiet, and answers,
when they come, are terse.

They speak in ecclesiastical terms
foreign to those not ensnared by
their zeal, dazzling and disorienting
at once. I long to be a part of such joy,

to soar like the regal birds they admire:
counting, cataloguing, exclaiming,
until it occurs to me that theirs
is just another doctrine of devotion,

their passion unique but ubiquitous:
they watch birds; my father collected
stamps; bakers swap recipes
and risen bread. All have their language,

their saints and sinners, hallelujahs
and amens; few are ecumenical enough
to see that, while the faces of their gods
differ, their call to worship is the same.

Chirp

Little is more hopeful than the sound
of peepers, the joy of amphibian
resurrection after the deep freeze
of winter. They seem to rouse at once,
a full-throated chirping chorus
in the marsh, their symphony bidding
us to shed the shroud of hibernation
and embrace the coming spring.

One morning on Davis Run

I discovered one sad, gray time in my life
that blue herons make excellent companions.
I was sitting on the bank of a rushing creek

that flows into the Bullpasture River. Spring,
and I was seeking some seasonal charm
to erase the chilling imprint of winter,

so I took myself there daily, nursing
the twin talismans of solitude and hope,
drawing comfort from new shoots of green,

the shush of rushing water—and then
one daybreak, there he stood, a tower
on spindly legs with a regal gaze.

Well, hello, I whispered. *You're early this year.*
He seemed unsure, but I comforted him.
It's OK, I said, *I'm looking for nourishment, too.*

He settled in, and we waited as one,
though I couldn't say for how long,
only that, as we grew accustomed

to our company, we shared the stream,
the golden magenta of an April dawn
and the kind of communion

that lifted me on outstretched wings
as he unfolded and, with ponderous flight,
took himself over the trees beyond.

On Shenandoah Mountain

In memory of Donald McCaig

That tall pine snag disappeared
from the ridge Sunday. It was felled
by the wind: a final surrender
after years of loss. Its limbs,
covered with lichen, withered
and dropped long ago, bark
scarred by deer and bear. Stubborn,
it stood. An elder of the woods,
it loomed above the seedlings
surrounding its base until the storm;
until, brittle, it tipped and fell,
shattered, scattered in pieces
on the ground. It was a grand old tree.
I miss its silhouette against the sky.

Turkey vulture
Cathartes aura

Sometimes, I wonder if they angered God,
if once they had been his most regal birds,
guardians of a high and holy place
until some sin, a mighty fall from grace,
for which he stripped their scarlet feather crowns
and cast them out to scavenge on the ground,
condemning them to feed upon the dead
with rheumy eyes and hideous red heads.
But when I watch them sail or dive and swoop,
or see the reverent air with which they roost,
I think upon their haj, their pilgrimage,
from Pharisees to lowly penitents:
modest monks in robes of chestnut brown.
outstretched wings in worship of the dawn.

Primal song

My neighbor traps and shoots, then hangs
coyotes on the branch of an old elm at the road,
once-savage bodies swinging in the sun.

It is an angry tableau, retribution
for tiny lambs stalked and eviscerated:
innocence shredded, tooth and bone.

His ritual does not stop the predators.
They attack his young to feed their own,
snug in dens nearby.

I've never told him I despise his grisly scene,
his vengeance near as frightening
as the shadows lurking in his herd.

And I've never said I listen for their howls
beneath the moon, thrill to hear their voices
in the deep December dark.

I cannot tell him of the fierce joy I feel
when they begin to sing, how their piercing,
wavering voices summon wildness deep within.

Opossum

They said the truest mercy
would be to shoot it dead.
I could not.

I'd seen it limp into the cool grass
beneath the autumn olive,
drag itself into a bloody knot

and settle, quietly, to die.
I called the dogs away,
shut them inside

and loaded bits of food
instead of bullets, laying my offering
among the roots.

It was gone next day, flat nest
abandoned for the woods
where coyote howls

announced fresh kill in the night.
I found the remnants later,
silver fur and bone among the leaves

my victim of kindness
delivered to agonizing end
because I could not.

Cardinal flower

You can find it now, down
past the meadow in the woods
where the creek turns, mud black
as pitch. Fight your way through
the brush or find a game trail
strong with the acrid cologne
of deer piss. Crouch, approach
with stealth, a thief.
True, it's going nowhere,

but hummingbirds, intent
on nectar from the tender
blossom of the cardinal flower,
will flee as you approach,
and you don't want to miss
the neon of their ruby throats
stretched taut to thrust
their needle beaks deep
inside its scarlet bloom.

Disciples

Dawn is but a promise when we wake,
but the birds hold fast to that vow
and sing happy, discordant hymns.
Our golden lights spill onto the marsh,
the water beyond slick as an otter's coat.

Murmuring, we make our way to the dock
breaking reverie with thumping oars,
rattling tackle and outboard roar,
off to meet the sun at Neal's Creek.

There, we flick, flick our flies
casting tiny, feathered prayers
to coax the wise one from the deep,
for we know he waits there.

We have not seen him,
but he has roused us this morning
and countless dawns before
when we have watched his spins and rolls and once,
we are sure, his shadow, the graceful swish
of his fanned tail stirring duckweed fronds below.

That lure is more powerful than any we hold,
and we come as though called. Steadfast,
reverent, we cast our offerings day after day,
unsure of our hope, both wishing and not
that he would rise to our bait.

When a tree falls

We know now that the answer is yes.
Though we are not present to hear
the noise in the forest, we have
learned it does make a sound,
heard and grieved by its sylvan family,
roots and rhizomes spreading
the tragic word that an elder has toppled,
that a hole is rent in the canopy
and the wisdom of seasons is gone.

Evangel

I never cease to be amazed
as we pause atop Shenandoah Mountain
gasping at the rolling Blue Ridge fading
in distant haze, never cease to be confounded
by what I find each time I break away
from that view and discover,
propped on the toilet paper dispenser
in the National Forest outhouse, a tract
beckoning me to follow Jesus.

I wonder about the disciples who think it
their ministry to spread the word there,
to speak of forgiveness, of holiness in air
thick with the smell of dung, to proselytize
by proxy, praying, I suppose, that those
seeing to one need might come to realize
another. Is this what Jesus meant when he said
his followers should be fishers of men?

I can't shake the pure wonder of those
who think to witness in a toilet, who want me
to pee and pray and emerge a new person
as the outhouse door closes with a thud
on an old way of life, and proclaim,
gazing across the mountain range beyond,
Mine eyes have seen the glory,
as though it wasn't evident before.

Lepidoptera

It rained today, a perfect summer shower
less storm than gift, with drops so fine
they seemed like silken threads unspooling
from the sky, calling us to be washed clean
by the whispering calm.
          Then came the butterfly.

Buffeted like a little boat at sea,
it was bouncing and beaten,
raindrops heavy on fragile Monarch wings.
Still, it plowed ahead until it found shelter
beneath the broad leaves of a milkweed,
where it folded and docked
until the storm moved on.

It held as brilliant sunshine backlit droplets
on the meadow, a silhouette in limp relief
against the rising steam.
A breeze ruffed the grass, and it stirred.
Carefully, it crept around
the milkweed's fat, lavender bloom
pausing atop to flex its wings.
Open and close, open and close,
a sunny, warming work delicate as a dance
until, sudden as the storm, it lifted, staggered,
and fluttered away.

Summer dawn

The sun, still searching for its magenta mask,
hasn't climbed from beneath the Outer Banks,
but word of its coming has chased the darkness to gray
and Currituck is yet slick water.
Silence, save crickets and chattering birds, hangs like drifting fog

until we hear the whine.
Soon there is another
and another.
Now a chorus of outboards sings across the glassy surface
skimming off to the distant Narrows.

We are still abed these mornings, but we hear them,
fishermen in their wooden boats, out to claim another day.
Drowsily, we follow their song
until the whine fades to the far off
and lulls us back to the cool of a linen pillow
and the sleep of an August dawn.

Cloister walk

The woods are still but for a twirling leaf
dangling by a single spider thread,
thin cousin to the dew-soaked cobwebs strewn
like silver mats across the forest floor.

A hidden choir of towhee, hawk and jay
performs a raucous descant from above.
Wet leaves and moss cushion rotting logs
that line my path.

Turkey scatter in a panic of squawks
and gobbles before silence envelops
anew and I sink into the dank embrace
of dark trees and chartreuse leaves
against a cloudless sky.

Blue moon

My friend feels sorry for the moon,
thinks it's overlooked
in favor of the gaudy brilliance
of the sun, which, she points out,
rises and sets, dawn to dusk,
while the moon, begrudgingly
allowed to *rise*, receives no
special notice when it vanishes
quietly into the pink morn or
decides to make an early
appearance even as the afternoon
sun glares pretentiously
and fights its appointed hour
to hand over the reins
with a psychedelic tantrum
of oranges and reds. *Well,*
I say, *We do, at least, name
the moons: Harvest Moon,
Hunter's Moon, Wolf Moon,
even,* I point out, *Blue Moon!*
She sighs, shakes her head.
Yes, she says. *Blue.*
My point, exactly.

With the dogs in the woods

They are canine docents
for an arboreal exhibit
I can scarcely behold.
Four-legged forensic
scientists, they parse
the smallest iota of odor
from sticks, leaves, or lichen,
my archaeologists of scent.

A paw print sends them
into a frenzy, then demands
they leave their own marks.
On they race, noses down,
logging a census of the past,
unaware of those who'll come
in our track: cautious wild things
gathering evidence of our passing,
sifting notes from the pungent
polyphony in our wake.

Hummingbird migration

She's been sitting on the feeder
since first light, gathering herself,
I suppose, for the journey south.
I wonder if she slept there, waking
for a sip from time to time, adding
calories, planning her long, winged
trek through the mountains to the Gulf
and across the waters to Mexico.

Not for the first time do I consider
the courage of the hummingbird
at one-tenth of an ounce, the toll
it will take to travel 3,000 miles
to flee the cold of winter. Not
for the first time do I consider
the family she fed and raised,
protecting her little ones from
predators bent on death.

It is the first time I consider her lucky.
She will travel alone. She will not
shepherd her children along the way,
coax them to walk through a desert
or push them over mountains; she will
not dry tears of exhaustion, ration
dwindling food or wrap them
in sheltering arms to keep out the cold.

She will not have them ripped
from those arms the moment
she reaches the haven she sought.

Tectonic

My friend the geologist
doesn't understand.
Why poetry? he asks,
*Why not write something
people actually read?*

All I could think was,
*Why stone? Why not
study something living,
breathing, alive!*
Instead, I smiled.

*Poems and rocks
are not so different,* I told him,
*both are metamorphic:
shaped by heat and pressure,
shifts of the earth—and time.*

Hawk

Its ease on the wind makes me
wonder whether it soars with joy
or simply views its flight
in the same ordinary way
I put one foot before the other
here on solid ground; whether,
when it sees me cross the meadow,
it pities my gravity as deeply as I yearn
to sail a limitless sky. I suspect not.
I suspect its eye is on a squirrel
or a rabbit, even as, breathless,
I follow the ferocious grace of its drift
and dive, with reverence that stills
my pedestrian gait.

Courtship

The handsome buck nibbles at meadow's edge,
idle, fat knees on muscular legs that hold
a golden body and a head bowed beneath
the weight of antlers.

A doe wanders nearby, grazing at the verge
until the buck stops to woo this delicate creature.
All strength and grace, he ambles her way
to lay claim.

Unperturbed, she snatches at the grass until he snorts.
Slowly, she lifts her head. She eyes him carefully,
then turns and, one languid step at a time, moves
into the undergrowth to vanish.

Nighthawks

Edward Hopper, Gallery 262, Art Institute of Chicago

When nighthawks strafed the meadow last night,
it reminded me of yours, of those lonely people
at the diner counter, separate but together,
sealed in melancholy, bathed in artificial light.

There's none of that here, where nighthawks
are known as Fair Birds because they arrive
just before the Ferris wheel and bumper cars,
swooping legions a-twirl at twilight, sudden,

then gone. We are joyous for the promise
they bring: crisping nights of fall, brilliant leaves.
In free, rambunctious flight, our nighthawks
sail on seas of grass, unencumbered

by any artist's frame like that fencing yours,
and I wonder: did your Nighthawks come
freely, or were they captured, posed
and frozen for your exhibit of despair?

When our nighthawks return this year
to pirouette and dive, we will feel
the heat of August take wing.
We will hear them buzz and cluck

and, if we listen closely, perhaps, a call
to join them—to climb off our stools,
abandon our seats at your counter,
and soar into the night.

Bird call

I heard my loon last night.
Just as the pink gray of dusk
settled on the mountain,
its querulous voice
filtered through the leaves
to announce its return.

I am sure it is the same bird
I hear each August. I have
decreed it so, just as I resist
its name, *Common Loon*,
as though there is something
ordinary about that voice,
its ebony beak, or crisp
black and white feathers
punctuated by vermillion eyes.

It settles on the river.
singular in its search
for solitude deep in the gorge
and I fall silent as it swims
and calls, swims and calls
gathering itself, beckoning me,
as we both summon strength
for the season yet to come.

Seeking relief

The Sierra Club mails me a quarter and says, with this,
they can save a wolf. Food for The Poor sends six cents.

That's all it takes, they tell me, *to feed a child for a day!*
I yell at the weighted envelopes, wonder about the pennies,

nickels and quarters wasted, the wolf sacrificed,
the hungry child doing without, just to induce my guilt.

They want me to send the money back, of course, add some
of my own, but it sits on my counter, tipping the scales

of good intentions with the force of frustration as I shrink
from the cost—*Pennies a day!*—of a lost and hungry world.

Provision

I found the fawn at sunrise
gutted and splayed, a pitiful tableau
by the creek; the most fragile of creatures
ambushed, parsed, then abandoned,
lifeless eyes agape.

I had heard the howl at night,
a coyote mother's hosanna
for the plenty provided her pups
in a den nearby, and it was easy
to despise her savagery.

That was before. Before I felt
the weight of need from my own
young. Before I confronted bellies
that ached from hunger grown
beyond my breasts. Before
I hunted fawns, myself.

In the wake of the storm

The woods are still as a vacant church.
Snow-covered ground sleeps beneath
leafless limbs draped in white.
Even the birds are quiet.

Our voices magnify the emptiness;
each booted print is a sacrilege,
but we are powerless agains the pull
to move deeper into the delicate sanctity

left by the storm, unable to quit lest we miss
the gift of calm in the wake of a blizzard
that buried our world in a crystalline quilt.
We celebrate its end and a new beginning

plowing ahead, knee-deep in white
beneath the stark renewal of a brilliant sky
and the distant cry of a hawk hunting
breakfast on a February day.

Pogonip

—a meteorological term
coined by Native Americans
to describe frozen fog.

Each limb and leaf
sprouts its own
chandelier
of frozen crystals,
singular threads
knitting an icy mantle
to drape
the ridge in white
beneath
the blush of dawn.

Skunk cabbage
Symplocarpus foetidus

He took me to the creek in search of hope.
I was wrapped in winter's deadening shawl,
and he was reaching for a single thread
to unravel the gray shroud of my despair.
It was, I warned him, ludicrous to think
that we could find renewal in these woods
combing frozen ground for tender shoots
of plants that stink of death to signal life.
Fetid by their very name, I said.
Still, we hunted, scouring icy leaves
along that bank of musk and cold decay,
until, at once, we saw them poking through:
chubby chartreuse pods of red and gold,
defiant signs of rebirth taking hold.

Threshold

Late February, and I sift
even the faintest sunbeam
for a signal that spring waits
to pry winter from my throat.
I am not without hope.

Yesterday, bluebirds returned,
two robins, then vultures
cruising on wind: birds of death
presaging the resurrection of life.
Today, I drop to my knees

in the bog, pull icy leaves
from the prehistoric finger
of a skunk cabbage sprout,
fearless first growth of the year.
Wet and cold, I turn home

along trails where violets and iris
slumber deep in frozen dirt,
coiled and waiting to emerge.
Patience, I whisper. Yes, we hear
goldfinch, nuthatch, the raucous laugh

of woodpeckers among the naked trees,
but you must not arise from your beds.
Wait, instead, for hummingbirds
to hover on soft air, for whippoorwills'
haunting calls at dusk and dawn.

Then, you can stand and blossom
and we will sing together
that winter is no more.

Benediction

The doctors are unflinching
in their diagnosis of his ills,
devising an intricate battle plan,
their full arsenal unleashed.
I have weapons of my own.

Today, I visit the Bullpasture River,
offering in hand, to show gratitude
for answered prayers during this war,
when many an *Amen* has been punctuated
by an eagle soaring in the mountain air.

A Blackfeet elder said I should honor
these birds, sent by The Creator,
by embracing their message of hope
and strength. He told me what to bring
and how to leave my gifts, but freed me
to follow the liturgy of my tradition

and so I kneel, gray sky spitting snow,
to place tobacco, berries, and fish
in wet leaves beside the rushing water.
I stare at my little pile of thanksgiving
and close my eyes to utter a prayer,
but all that emerges is a sigh.

Priscilla Melchior is a former community newspaper journalist who began writing poetry in 2013. Though reared in eastern North Carolina, she is a native of Virginia and retired there in 2011 intent on training her beloved border collies to be herding dogs. Life had other plans, though, and as she returned to writing, she found a new passion in poetry, often recalling the words of Sam Ragan, former newspaper editor and Poet Laureate of North Carolina. During her interview with him many years ago, he explained how a journalist may well have a poet inside. "There's not a lot of difference between writing for newspapers and writing poetry," he said. "Both forms require keen observation, strong descriptions, active verbs, and tight composition."

Her work has appeared in the *North Carolina Literary Review, Ekphrastic Review, Verse-Virtual* and *Streetlight Magazine,* among others. She is a Pushcart Prize nominee and has won a pair of awards from the Poetry Society of Virginia.